Grassland

Contents

Features

PROFILE

Turn to page 13 to read about Laura Ingalls Wilder and her much-loved stories set on the prairies.

MY DIARY

Imagine going on safari! Read the diary of a person who does in **On Safari** on page 22.

WORD BUILDER

What on Earth is a rufous hornero? Find out how this bird got its name on page 27.

IN THE NEWS

Read how green grasslands turned into deadly dust in **Storms Strike the Dust Bowl Again!** on page 29.

SITESEEING · PLANTS & ANIMALS ·

Why do zebras live in herds?

Visit **www.infosteps.co.uk** for more about **GRASSLAND ANIMALS.**

Grass, Grass, Grass!

Grass grows in most places on Earth. Large areas of land that are covered in grass with only a few scattered trees are called grasslands. Grasslands are found in areas that get more rain than deserts but less rain than forests. Grass is tougher than trees! It loses less water than tall plants, so it can grow in many places that trees can't.

Both large and small animals make their homes on grasslands around the world. Many people also live on grasslands, either on farms or in cities.

Grasses can regrow quickly after being burned, trampled, cleared, cut or eaten because the growing part of the grass plant is safely underground.

Grasslands of the World

About one-quarter of Earth's land is covered in grassland. There are two main kinds of grassland, **tropical** and **temperate**. Tropical grasslands, called savannahs, are found near the equator. Prairies, steppes and pampas are all temperate grasslands.

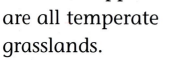

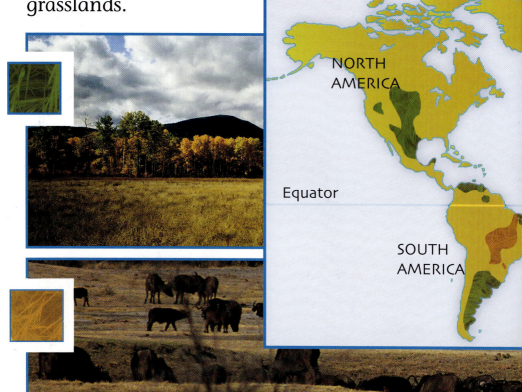

NORTH AMERICA

Equator

SOUTH AMERICA

There are about 10,000 different kinds of grass in the world. Some grasses, such as big bluestream grass, grow best in moist areas. Others, like June grass, grow better in drier areas.

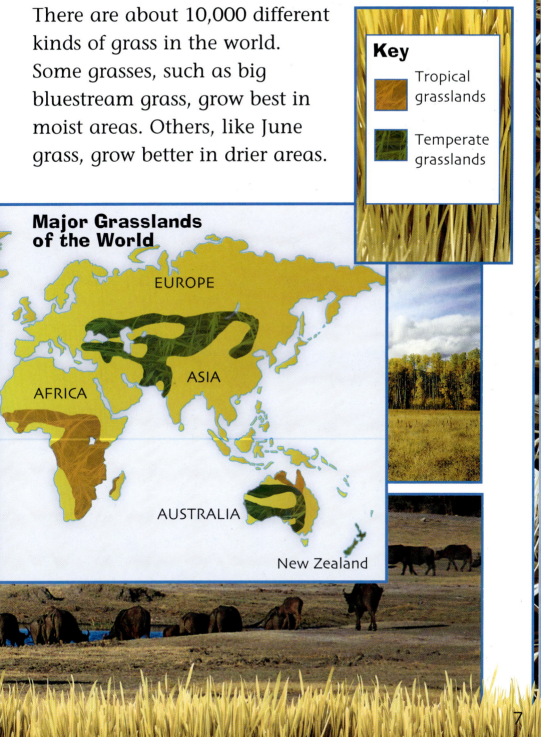

Key

Tropical grasslands

Temperate grasslands

Major Grasslands of the World

EUROPE

ASIA

AFRICA

AUSTRALIA

New Zealand

Prairies

Prairies are temperate grasslands, often with tall grass. Summers are hot on prairies, with temperatures reaching up to 38 degrees Celsius. Winters are cool and temperatures can drop to -40 degrees Celsius. Seasonal drought, natural fires and grazing by large **herbivores** prevent woody shrubs and trees from growing on prairie grasslands.

The Canterbury Plains, in New Zealand, are prairies. Most of the area is now used as farmland.

The North American prairies stretch from central Texas in the United States to southern Saskatchewan in Canada. This area is the largest grassland in the world. Many people as well as many kinds of animals make their homes on this great prairie.

Animals of the Prairies

Every animal of the North American prairies has its own special part to play in the prairie **ecosystem**. From the largest bison to the tiniest insect, every animal has an effect on the other plants and animals in the area.

Prairie dogs, meadowlarks and burrowing owls eat insects and grasses.

Burrowing owls make their nests in abandoned prairie dog burrows.

Prairie dogs live in large colonies called towns. Each town can have from 50 to 100 burrows. The prairie dogs' burrows are very important to life on the prairies. However, many farmers shoot or poison prairie dogs because they fear that their **stock** might step in burrow holes and break their legs.

Patches of grass eaten by deer and bison make it easier for prairie dogs and birds to see insects.

Prairie dogs mix the topsoil and the dirt below, making it easier for new grass to grow.

People of the Prairies

When the pioneers first saw the prairies of North America, they described them as "a sea of grass". Almost half of the United States was once grassland, but today little of the prairie remains untouched. Most of it has been turned into farms, ranches and cities.

The North American prairies are also a major source of coal, oil, gas and **uranium**. However, when people mine these natural resources, they often destroy the grassland ecosystem.

Key
- Alberta
- Saskatchewan
- Manitoba

Canada

Canada's prairie provinces are Alberta, Saskatchewan and Manitoba.

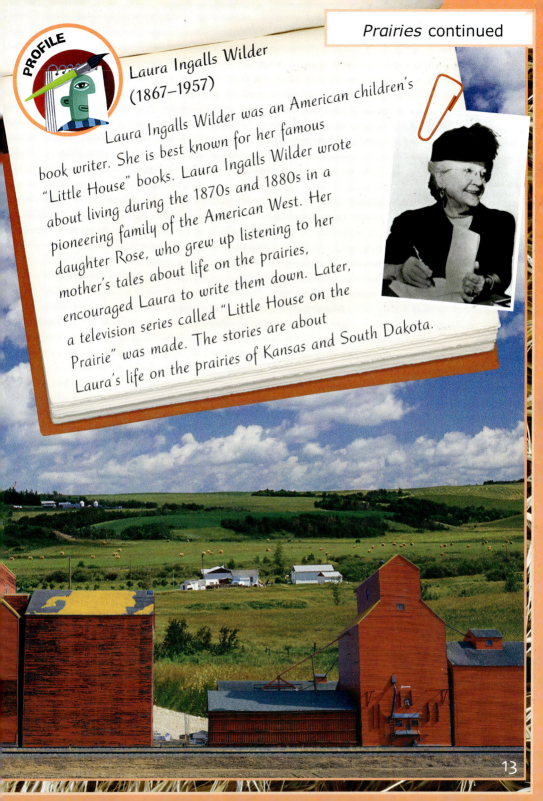

PROFILE

Laura Ingalls Wilder
(1867–1957)

Laura Ingalls Wilder was an American children's book writer. She is best known for her famous "Little House" books. Laura Ingalls Wilder wrote about living during the 1870s and 1880s in a pioneering family of the American West. Her daughter Rose, who grew up listening to her mother's tales about life on the prairies, encouraged Laura to write them down. Later, a television series called "Little House on the Prairie" was made. The stories are about Laura's life on the prairies of Kansas and South Dakota.

Carnivores such as lions and crocodiles attack the sick and weak members of the herds. **Scavengers** eat the leftovers from the carnivores' meals.

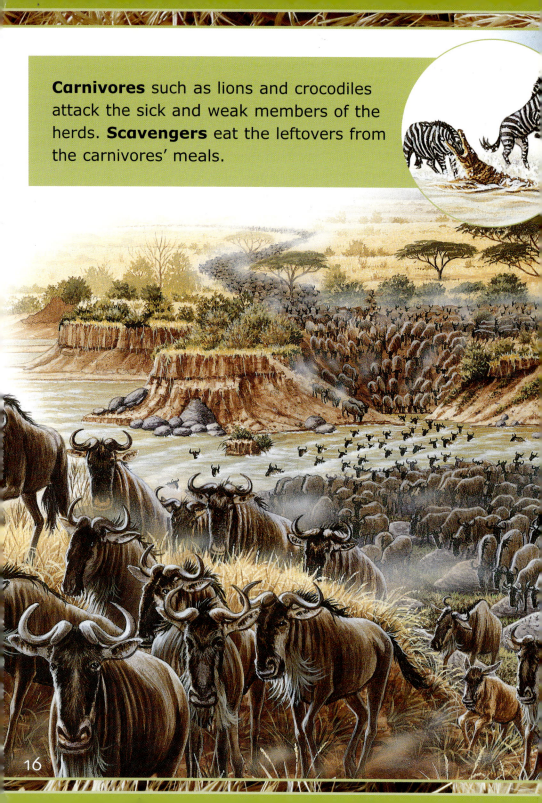

The Serengeti Plain

The Serengeti Plain is home to many large animals. Some of these animals graze on the grass, some eat the leaves from the few trees that grow on the savannah and some eat other animals.

When the dry season comes in June, over a million wildebeests and hundreds of thousands of zebras and antelopes move north in search of fresh grass and water. In November, they travel back again. This is called the Great Migration.

Wildebeests are the largest group of herbivores on the Serengeti. They are also the main food source for lions and hyenas.

Savannahs

Savannahs are tropical grasslands. There is a rainy season in summer and a drier season in winter. The drier season prevents too many trees from growing.

The Serengeti Plain in Africa is the biggest and best known savannah. There are also savannahs in Australia, India and South America.

Plant Protection

It is difficult for trees to grow in grasslands because the soil is often poor. Some trees, such as acacias, grow well on grasslands. Giraffes like to eat the leaves of acacia trees. However, if giraffes were to keep munching, they would eat the leaves faster than they could grow again.

Many
herbivores
live in
large herds
for safety.

17

AFRICA

Tanzania

The Great Migration

Key

- June
- July
- August–October
- November
- December–May

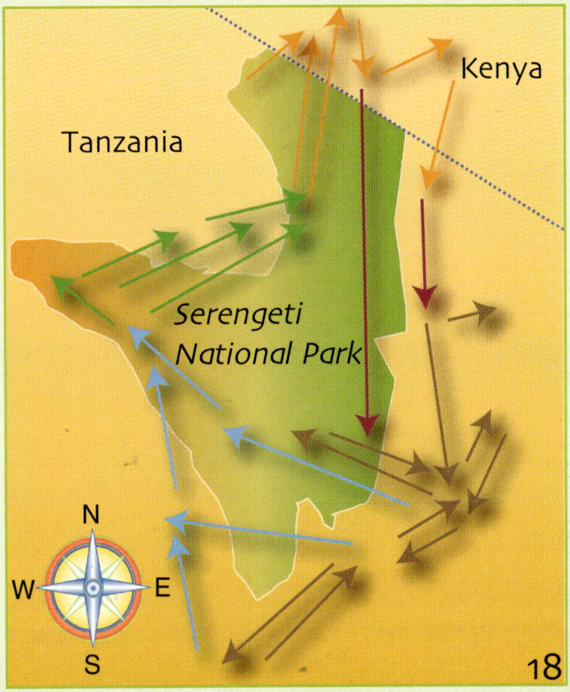

Tanzania

Kenya

Serengeti National Park

N
W E
S

18

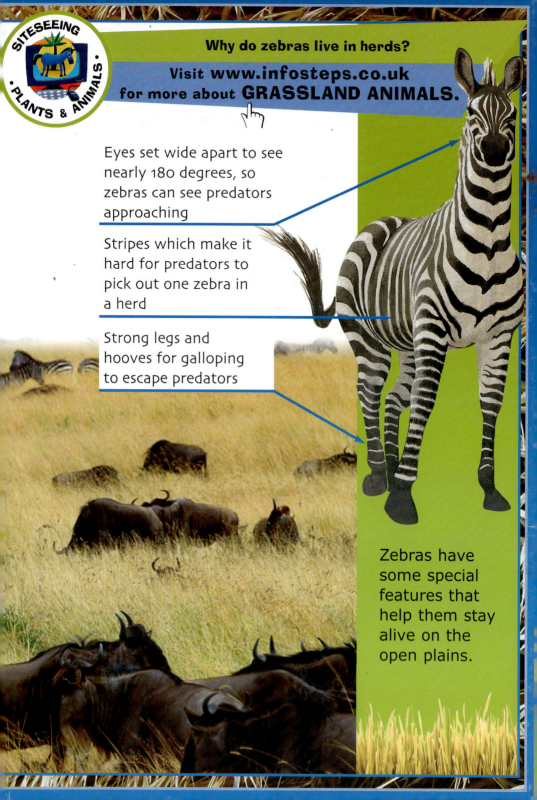

Why do zebras live in herds?

Visit **www.infosteps.co.uk** for more about **GRASSLAND ANIMALS.**

Eyes set wide apart to see nearly 180 degrees, so zebras can see predators approaching

Stripes which make it hard for predators to pick out one zebra in a herd

Strong legs and hooves for galloping to escape predators

Zebras have some special features that help them stay alive on the open plains.

So acacia trees protect themselves with toxic chemicals! When giraffes start to eat the leaves, the tree produces special chemicals that, after a while, make its leaves poisonous. This forces the giraffes to stop eating and move to another tree.

On Safari

Here we are in Tanzania. I'm writing this from our tent in a campground in the Serengeti National Park. Looking out through the tent flap, I can see three giraffes!

July 2

Our guide knows a lot about the wildlife of the savannah. He also told me that the word *safari* means "travel" in Swahili. Swahili is the language spoken by most people in East Africa.

July 5

We came across a pride of lions. Here's a picture of one of them. We spent ages watching them from the safety of our jeep. They're so used to people taking pictures of them, they didn't even seem to notice us!

July 7

We drove to a different part of the Serengeti today. The plains are home to huge herds of zebras and wildebeests, and we saw hundreds of these animals. I took some more great photos. It's amazing to see these wonderful animals in their natural **habitat.**

July 9

Our jeep nearly got stuck in deep mud as we drove through a shallow river to watch a herd of elephants. It's all part of the excitement on safari!

July 10

23

Steppes

Steppes are temperate grasslands like prairies. However, they are usually found in Europe and Central Asia. Steppes are often found between deserts and forests. They are warm in summer but very cold in winter.

Many of the animals that roam the steppes are herbivores such as horses, camels and antelopes. These animals usually live in herds for safety because there is little shelter on the steppes. Rabbits and other animals dig burrows for protection from predators.

The winter months on the steppes are very cold
so Bactrian camels grow long shaggy hair to stay warm.

Pampas

Pampas are great plains in South America. One region of Argentina is even called La Pampa. Pampas have good soil that is used for growing crops and farming animals. Huge cattle ranches cover much of the pampas. Many cities, such as Buenos Aires, have also been built on the pampas. More than 11 million people live in Buenos Aires.

South American cowboys, known as gauchos, are famous symbols of the pampas. Many stories and poems celebrate the adventures of gauchos. In the past gauchos lived by herding cattle across the unfenced pampas. Today you are more likely to see a gaucho at a parade or a festival.

WORD BUILDER

The rufous hornero lives on the pampas. This bird gets its name from its unusual nest. Its nest looks like a bread oven! The Spanish word for baker is *hornero*. Rufous comes from the Latin word *rufus*, which means "red".

Grasslands Under Threat

Grassland habitats disappear when too many trees take root and grow so sometimes people protect grasslands by setting fire to them! Controlled fires destroy any trees or shrubs that have taken root. They help the grass grow better too.

When cattle eat too much of the grass, grasslands can turn into deserts. Strong winds can then cause large dust storms. Many farmers are now careful to make sure that their grasslands stay in healthy shape by limiting the number of stock eating grasses.

May, 1936

Storms Strike the Dust Bowl Again!

Skies darkened again this afternoon as another severe dust storm swept across the plains.

Farms and houses were buried deep beneath layers of dirt and sand. Scientists believe that the dust storms are caused by drought and poor farming. The grasses that once held the soil in place have been dug up to make way for crops. Now, when strong winds blow across the plains, they whip the loose dirt into the air.

The Dust Bowl is an area in the United States that had a series of terrible dust storms in the 1930s. The dust storms lasted for ten years, destroying many farms and families.

Glossary

carnivore – an animal that eats meat

ecosystem – a community of plants and animals interacting with their environment

habitat – the natural home of an animal or a plant

herbivore – an animal that eats plants

scavenger – an animal that eats the leftovers of animals killed by predators. Hyenas and vultures are scavengers.

stock – cattle, sheep, pigs and other animals kept on a farm

temperate – a word that describes a place that is not too hot and not too cold

tropical – a word that describes what it is like in places that are in the Tropics. The Tropics are not far from the equator. Tropical places are hot and wet.

uranium – a silver-white metal which is used to produce nuclear power

Index

Lappet-faced vulture

Discussion Starters

1 Imagine you are going on safari to a grassland. Plan your trip. What animals would you like to see? What countries would you visit?

2 If something happens to one plant or animal in an ecosystem, it affects all the other plants and animals. What plants and animals would be affected if prairie dogs became extinct?

3 How does grass help prevent dust storms? What can people do to protect grasslands and prevent dust storms like those of the 1930s from happening again?